P9-CFA-587

Dance Me, Daddy

Written by award-winning
singer and songwriter

Cindy Morgan

illustrated by

Philomena O'Neill

ZONDER**kidz**

ZONDERVAN.com/
AUTHOR**TRACKER**
follow your favorite authors

Every good gift and every perfect gift is from above,
and comes down from the Father of lights,
with whom there is no variation or shadow of turning.
—James 1:17

To Olivia, Savannah, and Sigmund;
I hope we always dance in our living room.
~C.M.

To my dancing daughter Emma,
with much love.

~P.O.N.

Zonderkidz

Dance Me, Daddy
Copyright © 2009 by Cindy Morgan
Illustrations © 2009 by Philomena O'Neill

Requests for information should be addressed to:
Zonderkidz, Grand Rapids, Michigan 49530

Library of Congress Cataloging-in-Publication Data

Morgan, Cindy, 1968-
Dance me, daddy / by Cindy Morgan.
    p. cm.
  ISBN 978-0-310-71762-1 (hardcover)
1. Fathers and daughters--Juvenile literature. I. Title.
BF723.P25M67 2010
306.874'2--dc22
                              2008041516

Editor: Betsy Flikkema
Art direction & design: Sarah Molegraaf

Printed in the United States of America

10 11 12 13 14 LP/WPR 7 6 5 4 3

"King of the World" song lyrics

Spinning around on the tops of his feet.
Smiles of the angels could not be so sweet.
Wide blue eyes and piggy tails swirl.
She's her daddy's girl.

'Cause he knows the jokes that always make her laugh.
Takes her for ice cream instead of her nap.
At the end of the day by the light of moon they
Turn up the music in their living room.

And she yells, "Dance me. Dance me around till my feet don't ever touch down.
There's nothing better than being your girl.
And if I am your princess then, Daddy, you are the King of the World."

It's funny how life moves in circles of time.
To think not so long ago that face was mine.
Houses get smaller, we take different names,
But some things in life stay the same.

Some day she'll go off and find a life of her own
And marry a good man and make a happy home.
Until she comes back and sees with those same eyes what time cannot disguise.

She walks through the door with that look on her face,
'Cause Daddy's brown hair has all turned to gray.
They talk for hours.
They cry and they laugh.

Watching old movies and thinking back.
Just as she turns to go, she says,
"Hey, Dad, how about one for the road?

"Dance me. Dance me around till my feet don't ever touch down.
Dance me. Dance me around till my feet don't ever touch down.
'Cause there's nothing better than being your girl. Oh, no,
there's nothing better than being your girl.
And if I am your princess then, Daddy,
you are the King of the World,
King of the World."
Spinning around on the tops of his feet.
Smiles of the angels could not be so sweet.

Spinning around on the tops of his feet, she smiles like an angel and looks up so sweet. She wears a princess gown and a cardboard crown, and her piggy tails dance and swirl. He's her hero brave and strong, and she's her daddy's girl.

He tells her jokes and makes her laugh. They
play I spy, let's pretend, and catch me if you can.

When the moon is out and the sun is asleep,
after dinner, dessert, and bedtime stories,
she climbs up on the tops of his feet and says . . .

"Dance me, Daddy. Dance me around.
Don't let my feet ever touch down.
There's nothing better than being your girl.
If I am your princess, then you are king of the world."

Days turn to years, and his little girl grows.
She packs away princess gowns and crowns and bows.
She meets new friends and wears different clothes.

Sometimes when she's sleeping, he kneels by her bed
to pray that her Father in heaven is watching over her
every moment of every day.

Even though some things change,
some things stay the same.

When the moon is out and the sun is asleep, after dinner, homework, and a little TV, they turn up the music and in his arms she swings.

"Dance me, Daddy. Dance me around.
Don't let my feet ever touch down.
There's nothing better than being your girl.
If I am your princess, then you are king of the world."

One day her daddy waves good-bye. He always knew this day would come, when his little girl would be all grown up, when she'd go off to see the world, meet a boy, and fall in love.

Her wedding day arrives, and the church bells chime.
In her white princess gown she smiles that same smile.

And even though some things change,
some things stay the same.

By the light of the moon and that same sweet song,
she steps into her daddy's arms before the moment is gone.

"Dance me, Daddy. Dance me around.
Don't let my feet ever touch down.
There's nothing better than being your girl.
If I am your princess, then you are king of the world."